Slumbering Giants

The volcanoes and thermal regions of the central North Island

Geoffrey J. Cox

HarperCollins*Publishers New Zealand*

Acknowledgements

My acknowledgements fall neatly into two camps. Firstly, I would like to thank the many hikers, campers and trampers who added spice to my two-week journey around the Taupo Volcanic Zone. In particular, my warmest thanks go to Jason Butterfield and Ernie Lober, who joined me for the four days spent climbing among and over the volcanoes of Tongariro National Park.

Secondly, I would like to thank the experts who shared their knowledge with me: Dr Les O. Kermode of the DSIR Geological Survey, Auckland; Dr C. Peter Wood of the DSIR Geological Survey, Rotorua; Beth A. Palmer of the Department of Soil Science, Massey University; and Simon Noble of the Department of Conservation, Tongariro National Park.

Finally, three people deserve special mention: My father, Ernie Cox, who proof-read the text and provided a valuable layman's viewpoint; my fiancée, Barbara Hochstein, whose blunt but constructive criticisms of the illustrations caused all to be altered and a few to be completely redone; and Professor Manfred P. Hochstein of the Geothermal Institute, University of Auckland, who read the text and corrected my misconceptions with unfailing patience.

First published 1989
Reprinted 1992, 1994, 1996

HarperCollins*Publishers (New Zealand) Limited*
P.O. Box 1, Auckland

Copyright © 1989 Geoffrey J. Cox

ISBN 1 86950 012 1

Production by Pages Literary Pursuits
Typeset by Typeset Graphics Ltd, Auckland
Printed and bound in Hong Kong

Cover: *A major eruption of Tongariro must be an awe-inspiring sight, yet this volcano is small compared to some in New Zealand. Here, Tongariro's North Crater is seen as it may have appeared in eruption about 10,000 years ago. It is viewed from what is now State Highway 47, due north of the mountain. The beech forest which today cloaks the lower slopes is absent for at this time the Ice Age had only recently passed its peak and much of the central North Island was above the tree line.*

Contents

The differing faces of the Volcanic Plateau exemplified by the two Tarawweras: below, the lake; above, the mountain.

Introduction

Running through the North Island of New Zealand is the geological equivalent of an open wound. It is over 240 kilometres long yet no more than 50 kilometres wide, and within its boundaries have occurred some of the most violent volcanic eruptions the world has known.

The results of this activity are impressive: a plateau of volcanic material rising about 500 metres above sea level and extending up to four kilometres below, which incorporates more than 20,000 cubic kilometres of volcanic rock; a landscape pockmarked with a mass of vast craters, many 15 kilometres or more in diameter, peppered with several hundred volcanic cones, including mountains up to 2797 metres high, and scattered with seventeen active geothermal regions.

Yet, paradoxically, this region is one of the most scenic in New Zealand, with deep, clear lakes nestling amidst forested hills, snow-capped mountain peaks rising above stark plains and, it must be said, seemingly endless pine plantations. A Mecca for fishermen, skiers, trampers and sight-seers, to the tourist it is the 'Volcanic Plateau', to the geologist the 'Taupo Volcanic Zone'.

1. A land under tension

The Taupo Volcanic Zone owes its existence to New Zealand's position astride the boundary of two of the earth's crustal plates.

The sunken continent

Despite appearances to the contrary, New Zealand is a continent almost half the size of Australia. It is, however, largely submerged by the sea, with only the high land — the three main islands, the Chatham Islands to the east and several small islands such as Campbell Island to the south — projecting above the water. Like all continents, it rests on the earth's *lithosphere*, a layer of denser rock about 100 kilometres thick. The lithosphere itself floats on the *asthenosphere*, a 200 kilometre-thick zone, chemically no different from the lithosphere but so hot (about 1400 to 1500°C) that its rocks are close to their melting point and are capable of plastic flow (that is, when placed under pressure, they deform like plasticine rather than breaking, as rocks nearer the surface do).

The lithosphere, which also lies beneath all the oceans of the world, is not a single, continuous layer, but is composed of about a dozen vast plates, some of which are thousands of kilometres across. Convection currents in the asthenosphere keep these plates moving at speeds of about five centimetres a year. Where plates are pulled apart, the lithosphere is stretched, asthenosphere ascends and melts, and the lighter portion (*magma*) rises through the lithosphere to form new sea floor. The zone of stretching is marked on the surface by a chain of sea floor volcanoes — the mid-ocean ridges.

Where two plates collide, the result depends upon the composition of the upper few kilometres (the crust) of each plate. There are two types of crust, a thicker (35 kilometres average), lighter, *continental type*, and a thinner (5 to 10 kilometres), heavier *oceanic type*. If two plates with continental crust collide, neither yields, although one may slide horizontally beneath the other. Enormous crumples develop along the collision zone, forming mountains, yet volcanism in this situation is extremely rare. The Alps and the Himalayas (where the African and the Australian-Indian plates respectively are colliding with the Eurasian Plate) are two examples of the results of such an impact.

Where both plates have oceanic crust, one generally slides beneath the other (is *subducted*) and plunges deep into the asthenosphere where, since the crust has a lower melting point than the surrounding rock, it melts. The resulting magma rises through fractures (*faults*) in the leading edge of the over-riding plate to erupt on the earth's surface as volcanoes, often forming an island chain adjacent to a deep ocean trench (which marks the place where the subducted plate begins its descent). The Tongan and Kermadec Islands and their adjacent trench are examples of this form of collision.

When a plate with continental crust collides with one with oceanic crust, the latter plate is subducted so that this time the volcanoes resulting from the melting of the oceanic crust form a string of volcanoes along the edge of the land mass, such as those of the Andes of South America. It is to this form of volcanism that the Taupo Volcanic Zone is related.

The New Zealand continent actually straddles the collision line between the Australian-Indian Plate and the Pacific Plate. The Macquarie, Kermadec and Tongan trenches and ridges mark the plate boundary south and north of the country, while New Zealand itself has been crumpled in the South Island to form the Southern Alps, and stretched in the North Island to form the Taupo Volcanic Zone.

Volcanoes and eruptions

The shape of a volcano is determined by the violence with which it erupts, which in turn is largely controlled by the gas content and viscosity of the *lava* (magma with most of the dissolved gases removed). The viscosity depends mainly upon the lava's silica and gas content, with a higher content of either resulting in a more viscous lava. In contrast, the most fluid lavas, called *basaltic* lava, have a low silica content. When cool, they are generally black in colour. They are formed from molten asthenosphere which has risen from deep below the surface.

Lavas with a moderate silica content are called *andesite* or *dacite*. Their rock is paler than basalt and comes, not from the asthenosphere, but from the molten upper layer of the subducted plate.

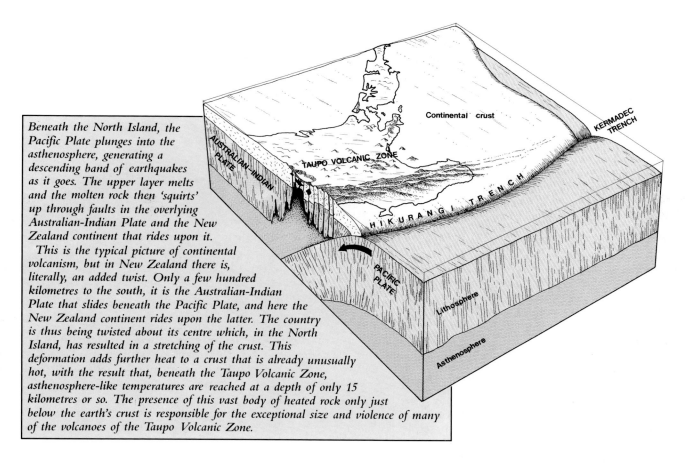

Beneath the North Island, the Pacific Plate plunges into the asthenosphere, generating a descending band of earthquakes as it goes. The upper layer melts and the molten rock then 'squirts' up through faults in the overlying Australian-Indian Plate and the New Zealand continent that rides upon it.

This is the typical picture of continental volcanism, but in New Zealand there is, literally, an added twist. Only a few hundred kilometres to the south, it is the Australian-Indian Plate that slides beneath the Pacific Plate, and here the New Zealand continent rides upon the latter. The country is thus being twisted about its centre which, in the North Island, has resulted in a stretching of the crust. This deformation adds further heat to a crust that is already unusually hot, with the result that, beneath the Taupo Volcanic Zone, asthenosphere-like temperatures are reached at a depth of only 15 kilometres or so. The presence of this vast body of heated rock only just below the earth's crust is responsible for the exceptional size and violence of many of the volcanoes of the Taupo Volcanic Zone.

Lavas with a very high silica content are called *rhyolite*. They are normally whitish or cream in colour and are composed largely of molten continental crust.

In the Taupo Volcanic Zone, all types of lava have occurred. In fact, many volcanoes have produced different types of lava with different eruptions. Mount Tarawera, for example, had produced only rhyolitic lava until it erupted basaltic lava in 1886.

Lava may issue from the volcano vent as a flow, but it may also be emitted in a variety of other forms. *Airfall material* is a term used to describe lava which is thrown from the volcano so violently that it solidifies before it hits the ground. It varies in size from fine *ash* (the principal constituent of the typical eruption cloud) to *scoria*, which may be of considerable size and is recognised by its rough texture, the entire rock being honeycombed with bubbles of gas that 'froze' in place as the lava splatters cooled in flight. Scoria may be black, grey or red in colour, the last being the result of oxidation while in flight.

Pyroclastic material generally issues from the volcano as a ground-hugging flow which contains an unsorted mixture of gas, lava fragments and solid blocks. Being very heavy yet, thanks to the gas content, almost friction free, it may travel at incredible speed. Many such flows eventually form a jumble of loose material but, if they are hot enough, the constitutions may be virtually molten and the flow cools to a solid rock, called *ignimbrite*.

Pumice is a common ingredient of pyroclastic flows in New Zealand. It is formed from the froth which can occur as rhyolitic magma nears the surface. Generally whitish in colour, the rock is so filled with air holes that it may actually float on water.

History of the region

A belt of volcanic activity has been moving southwards through the North Island for millions of years. This migration is probably the result of a slow southward movement of the eastern half of the North Island relative to the western part. About 20 million years ago, East Cape probably lay alongside Northland, but subsequently it slid southwards, leaving a string of progressively younger volcanoes in its wake. Thus, 15 million years ago, Great Barrier Island was in eruption and 10 million years later the most southerly volcanoes of the Coromandel peninsula were being created.

At the same time as it moved southwards, the eastern half of the North Island was being rotated clockwise, stretching the crust between the two halves and creating a rift in which, about two million years ago, volcanoes started

Volcanoes of the zone

The image of a volcano as a mountain with a crater in its summit requires modification in the Taupo Volcanic Zone. While such volcanoes exist, they are outnumbered by those which are either mountains without craters or craters without mountains.

Andesite/dacite volcanoes

These are the 'conventional' volcanoes of the zone, and as far as we are concerned the two can be considered identical. They are created when magma, largely derived from the melting of the Pacific Plate, rises through fissures from depths of 100 kilometres or more to create a magma chamber a few kilometres below the earth's surface. Some crustal rock is incorporated into the magma, generating gases as it melts, while the magma, too, gives off gases, the chief of which is water vapour. These eventually cause a rise in pressure in the chamber to a point where the weight of ground above can no longer contain it. The volcano erupts, building a cone of ejected material around the vent. Further eruptions occur whenever pressure in the magma chamber exceeds the weight of the material in the vent. Tongariro, Ruapehu and White Island are all andesite volcanoes.

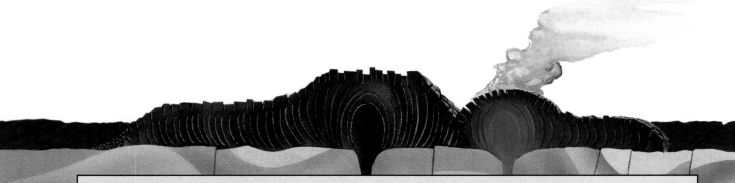

Rhyolite dome volcanoes

This is an unusual type of volcano that is, however, common in the Taupo Volcanic Zone. The eruption starts explosively, creating a vent. Up this the lava oozes, but it is so viscous that instead of spreading out over the surrounding land it remains intact, forming a steep-sided dome. Some minor flows may occur, but on the whole the growth of the volcano is caused by new lava welling up inside the dome, forcing the outer layers to expand upwards and outwards. Onion-like layers of cooling rock develop within the dome while, on the surface, deep, rubble-filled fissures form. If the lava is fluid enough, part of the volcano may slump and spread slightly under its own weight, but otherwise the result is a hill or mountain with a domed or flattish top. Typically, the crumbling of the outer layer of the volcano soon results in the development of a 'skirt' of loose stones from which the upper slopes project as steep cliffs.

A single eruption may last for several years but, once finished, the volcano rarely erupts again through the same vent. Generally, a new vent opens beside the dome in which another dome rises so that, ultimately, most large dome volcanoes are composed of a number of coalescing domes. Mount Tarawera, Mount Ngongotaha and Mokoia Island, in Lake Rotorua, are all rhyolite dome volcanoes.

Rhyolite caldera volcanoes

Dome volcanoes are the result of large-scale crustal melting at depths of only five to ten kilometres. However, because the resulting rhyolitic magma is both very viscous and very rich in gases, the slow eruption of dome volcanoes is not enough to release the pressure from a very large crustal melt. As a result, intervals of dome volcano building may be interspersed with cataclysmic pyroclastic eruptions when the magma chamber is rapidly and violently emptied.

Huge quantities — sometimes in excess of 100 cubic kilometres — are hurled into the sky in a matter of days. The eruption cloud can rise to 30 kilometres or more, depositing ash over all New Zealand. Hot avalanches of gas and lava, called pyroclastic flows, surge out from the vent across the surrounding land at speeds that are initially close to that of sound. Many hundreds of square kilometres of land around the vent may be covered in debris that can be more than 100 metres deep. As the flow cools, lava and ash may weld together, the extent of welding depending on the thickness and the original temperature of the flow. At one end of the scale, largely unwelded material is called

breccia; at the other is ignimbrite, a solid rock. More than 25,000 square kilometres of the central North Island are mantled by such rock.

As the eruption progresses, so much magma is ejected that the roof of the magma chamber collapses, forming a vast, shallow crater, called a caldera, which can be 20 kilometres across. After the eruption, the caldera often fills with water to form a lake that, should the volcano erupt again, will react with the hot magma, generating superheated steam which will increase still further the violence of the eruption (a phreato-magmatic eruption).

Lake Rotorua and Lake Taupo are both rhyolite caldera volcanoes. The former has had only one major period of eruption in its entire history while the latter (more typically) has erupted several times. However, many thousands of years separate such eruptions, each one of which created a new caldera. Between eruptions, caldera volcanoes appear deceptively tranquil, totally unlike most people's conception of a volcano — many have heard that Taupo was once an active volcano but few realise that it is today.

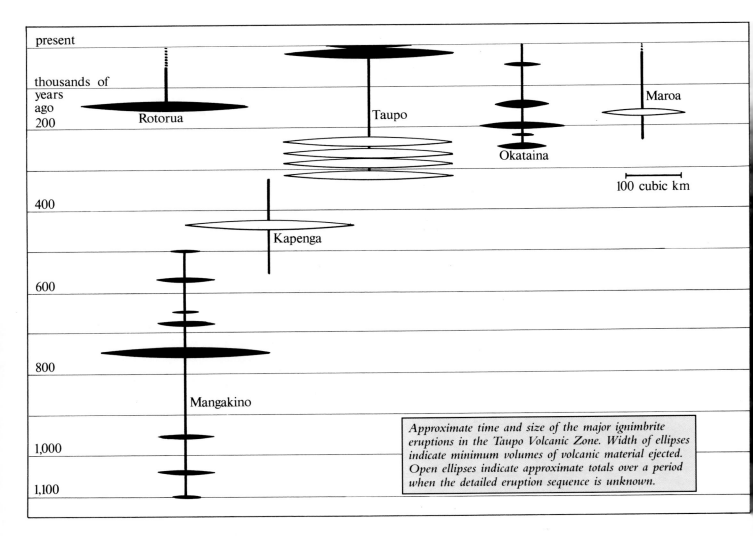

present

thousands of
years
ago
200

Rotorua

Taupo

Maroa

Okataina

100 cubic km

400

Kapenga

600

800

Mangakino

Approximate time and size of the major ignimbrite
eruptions in the Taupo Volcanic Zone. Width of ellipses
indicate minimum volumes of volcanic material ejected.
Open ellipses indicate approximate totals over a period
when the detailed eruption sequence is unknown.

1,000

1,100

rising. Today the oldest volcanoes in the Taupo Volcanic Zone such as Titiraupenga and Pureora (both almost two million years old) lie along the western margin of this rift while the youngest, such as Mount Edgecumbe and Tauhara, lie along the eastern side. Volcanoes of up to about a million years of age lie scattered between them.

Many more volcanoes lie in this central region than meet the eye. They have, however, been buried (despite the fact that some are probably as big as Ruapehu), for the entire area is covered to a depth of at least two kilometres in debris from pyroclastic eruptions. As fast as volcanoes have buried the land, so it has sunk. This sinking process is still continuing and can be surprisingly rapid. After a major earthquake in 1987, areas of the Taupo Volcanic Zone dropped by more than a metre.

The first ignimbrite eruption occurred less than two million years ago, and such cataclysmic eruptions have continued unabated ever since. Mangakino, the earliest ignimbrite volcanic centre, was probably at times overlaid

by a lake, as the Taupo centre is today. Time has obscured the details of Mangakino's life, but it is thought that one eruption is responsible for the ignimbrite layer that lies two to three metres deep in parts of Auckland, 170 kilometres away!

As at the Kapenga and Maroa volcanic centres, subsequent ignimbrite eruptions have buried the Mangakino caldera so deeply that little evidence now remains on the surface of this volcano. However, beneath the ground, magnetic surveys indicate that the thickness of volcanic rock overlying the continental crust increases to more than four kilometres — a feature common to all the volcanic centres.

Two centres, Taupo and Okataina, are considered to be still highly active. The last Taupo eruption was an ignimbrite eruption in 186 AD. Okataina's last rhyolitic eruption was only 700 years ago, when Mount Tarawera was formed. The 1886 eruption of that volcano was a basaltic eruption that used the fracture zone which Tarawera was built upon.

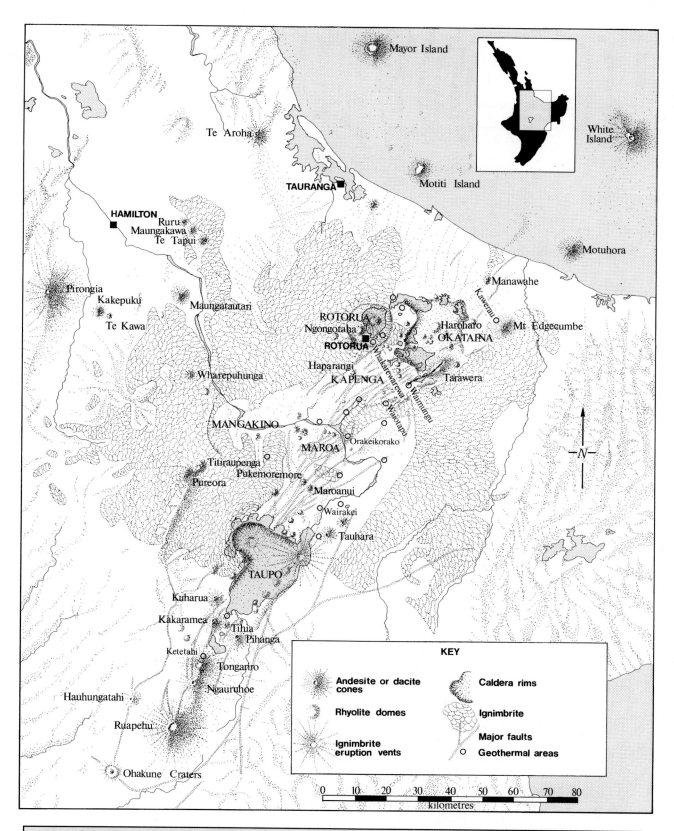

KEY

- ⬥ **Andesite or dacite cones**
- ⬥ **Rhyolite domes**
- ✳ **Ignimbrite eruption vents**
- **Caldera rims**
- **Ignimbrite**
- **Major faults**
- ○ **Geothermal areas**

0 10 20 30 40 50 60 70 80
kilometres

Map of the Taupo Volcanic Zone

Erosion has eaten deeply into the perimeter of the ignimbrite cover, while in the centre it is buried beneath the fallout of countless smaller eruptions. Volcanoes and faults are so numerous in the centre of the zone that only the most prominent have been shown here. To the

west and north lie a number of older cones which predate the formation of the Taupo Volcanic Zone. Beyond White Island are the Rumble Seamounts (not visible on this map), underwater volcanoes which trace the line of volcanic activity northwards to the Kermadec Islands and Tonga.

2. The greatest eruption on earth

In the late summer of 186 AD, Europe experienced a series of sunrises and sunsets so spectacular that more than one Roman historian was moved to record them for posterity. Eight thousand kilometres away, the Chinese were witnessing, and recording, a similar phenomenon: "During the reign of the Emperor Ling Ti (168–189 AD) several times the sun rose in the east red as blood and lacking light; only when it had risen to an elevation of more than two zhàng was there any brightness. When it set in the west, at two zhàng above the horizon it was similarly red...Also during this period, several times when the moon rose and set and was two to three zhàng above the horizon, all was red as blood."

What both these civilisations were seeing was probably an effect of the most violent eruption the world had known for 5000 years — that of Lake Taupo in New Zealand.

As far as Taupo was concerned, the eruption was nothing special — certainly it was far smaller than its last ignimbrite eruption

> The climax of the last eruption of Taupo came when, in no more than a few hours, 30 cubic kilometres of lava were hurled into the sky. The eruption cloud thus created collapsed under its own weight and a pyroclastic flow swept across the surrounding land. In this view, about 30 kilometres from the vent, the towering eruption cloud dominates the landscape while, much closer, the ground-hugging flow of hot gases and rock fragments approaches at a speed of several hundred kilometres an hour.

20,000 years previously. That eruption had thrown out more than 300 cubic kilometres of volcanic material, and buried all New Zealand in at least a centimetre of ash. What the latest eruption lacked in size, however, it more than made up in violence, earning Taupo the dubious distinction of being the most violent currently active volcano on earth.

Taupo is a rhyolite caldera volcano, and a number of vents lie beneath the bed of the present lake. Most are, however, so deeply buried beneath the debris of later eruptions that only the last vent, towards the north-eastern end of the lake, is still recognizable. The volcano has been erupting intermittently for the last 330,000 years, and there has been a lake in the caldera for at least 100,000 years. The early eruptive history is poorly known, but we can reconstruct events of the past 22,000 years in some detail.

Eruption 22,000 years ago

The eruption of 22,000 years ago was the first major ignimbrite eruption for more than 100,000 years. The presence of the lake greatly affected the course of events. The periodic introduction of large quantities of water into the vent caused enormous steam explosions which threw ash exceptionally high into the atmosphere so that, eventually, more than 10 per cent of the Southern Hemisphere received some ash fall. Moreover, the violence of the explosions pulverised the ejected material to a far smaller particle size than would otherwise have occurred, while the water cooled the pyroclastic flows so that, when solidified, they formed welded ignimbrite rock only immediately around the vent. The eruption was brief. In a matter of days more than 300 cubic kilometres of debris were produced that covered an area of 10,000 square kilometres, stretching up to 65 kilometres from the vent.

Eruption in 186 AD

Apparently exhausted by this effort, Taupo fell silent for 10,000 years. Then came a series of eight relatively small eruptions which built rhyolite domes and produced the occasional small pyroclastic flow. Today, these volcanoes form a line running across the eastern bed of the lake (Motutaiko Island and Horomatangi Reefs mark two of the eruption sites), then into the hills west of Taupo township and on to the north. Evidence suggests that all these eruptions occurred on dry land, so we must conclude that, at this time, the lake was confined to the western end of its present domain. It was the ninth eruption which created Lake Taupo as we know it today for, with that eruption, the volcano reverted to

type. Although no eruption anywhere in the world has since come close to the violence of the 186 AD eruption (despite the fact that two have produced as much or more material), analysis of the particle size and layering of the ejected material enables us to make an educated guess at the course of events.

Initially the eruption, while violent, affected only the immediate area. At first it seems that this vent, too, was above lake level, but subsidence soon occurred leading to violent explosions, as lake water flashed to steam, which threw up ash, scoria and lava, creating an impressive eruption cloud. The presence of so much water led to a very 'wet' eruption, and for some weeks the volcano showered the surrounding land with muddy ash, building up a layer many metres thick on the shores of the lake. So water-saturated was this deposit that run-off channels cut deeply into it as excess water drained back into the lake. Then the roof of the magma chamber subsided further, perhaps abruptly, and a huge volume of lake water rushed into the vent. The eruption immediately increased to an unprecedented level of violence.

In a period of no more than a day, more than 20 cubic kilometres of pumice, ash and rocks were ejected, forming a vast eruption cloud which probably reached a height of 50 kilometres. Prevailing winds carried this cloud far to the east to shed its load over the eastern North Island and the Pacific Ocean. Such was the fallout that, over the next few hours, 30,000 square kilometres were buried to a depth of at least 10 centimetres.

Then the violence of the eruption increased still further from the simply unbelievable to the almost inconceivable. In a matter of hours (one estimate suggests less than seven minutes) 30 cubic kilometres of volcanic material were hurled skywards, forming a cloud so heavy that it almost immediately collapsed under its own weight. A shock wave exploded outwards at the speed of sound, flattening forests and killing wildlife, and in its wake came a boiling pyroclastic flow. Forced on by the collapsing cloud behind it and rendered almost friction-free by the amount of gas within it, this poured over the ground at an initial speed close to that of sound, covering mountains, hills and valleys alike to a distance of 90 kilometres from the volcano. The flow even reached Red Crater on Tongariro, 400 metres above present Lake Taupo, although it failed to top Ruapehu. Any remaining lake water was turned to steam and incorporated in the flow, and wood was instantly carbonised as it was engulfed. The amount of water in the lake meant the pyroclastic flow, although over 300°C, was too

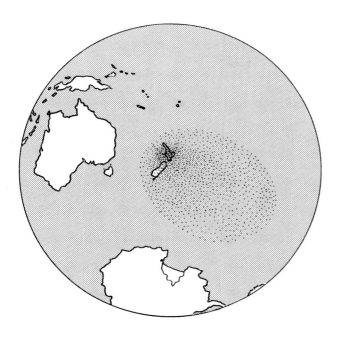

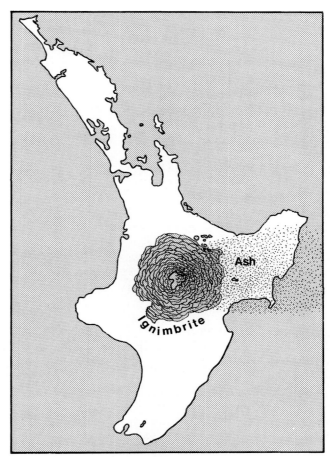

(above) *The Taupo eruption of 22,000 years ago rained ash down upon an estimated 10 per cent of the Southern Hemisphere. All New Zealand received at least one centimetre of ash; 12 centimetres fell on the Chatham Islands, 800 kilometres from the volcano.*

(right) *Distribution of ignimbrite and ash falls more than 10 centimetres thick following the Taupo eruption of 186 AD.*

cool to form ignimbrite rock save near its source, but the partially welded material formed a mantle more than 100 metres deep near the lake and blanketed 20,000 square kilometres of the surrounding land.

This stupendous explosion marked the end of the eruption. More than 110 cubic kilmometres of material had been ejected and the roof of the magma chamber collapsed completely, forming a wide caldera. The fine ash thrown so high into the air would, in time, spread throughout the world and cause the red sunsets the Chinese and Romans reported. The volcanic plateau, meanwhile, was left in peace to recover.

After the eruption the central North Island must have been a desolate place indeed. Apart from the gentle hiss of steam escaping from the cooling layer of ignimbrite, not a sound would have broken the utter silence of the devastated landscape while, even beyond the reach of the ignimbrite, heavy falls of toxic, suffocating ash killed forests, leaving many square kilometres of dead wood through which vast fires, started by lightning strikes, swept unimpeded. But this eerie world was short-lived for, even as close as 20 kilometres from the vent, some animal and plant life had survived, protected from the full

force of the eruption by high hills.

Within relatively few years, tussock, bracken and scrub had invaded the desert, encouraging insects and birds which, in turn, brought the seeds of larger plants. Soon, taller secondary vegetation was well established, providing the shade essential for the growth of the trees of a mature forest. Within 300 years, dense forest once more cloaked the shores of the rejuvenated lake, while, further out, the volcanic ash which had originally killed the trees now combined with the carbon from their burning to revitalise the soil, encouraging rapid regeneration.

It was, however, a different forest from its predecessor for the poorly-drained, nutrient-depleted soils of old now lay buried beneath metres of fast-draining pumice. Where before, rimu, beech and many hardwood trees had dominated, the new soil favoured matai and totara. Over the years, the new forest increased in complexity so that today, eighteen hundred years later, the casual observer would never realise the eruption had taken place.

Today, 'the most violent volcano on earth' presents a face of deceptive tranquillity as nothing more than the occasional squall disturbs its deep waters. Cutting through the

Ignimbrite, the solid rock which can form from a cooled pyroclastic flow, is common throughout the Taupo Volcanic Zone. Here, just downstream from the Maraetai Dam, the Waikato River has exposed just the upper part of the ignimbrite from an ancient eruption of either Taupo or Mangakino. The term 'ignimbrite' was coined in New Zealand to describe such welded flows in which vertical cracks formed as they cooled.

ignimbrite mantle and flowing into the lake are some of the finest trout streams in New Zealand, and this beautiful area is understandably popular with holiday-makers, who can enjoy not only fishing but also boating and hiking. Thermal regions, scattered along the lake shore, are seen as an added attraction rather than as a hint of the mighty forces that lie dormant below. But deep under the lake bed is still an ominous hot spot. The world has not heard the last of the Taupo volcano!

Karapiti geothermal area (Craters of the Moon)

Just north of Lake Taupo, close to State Highway 1, lies Karapiti, a spectacular geothermal area of violently eruptive mudpools and fumaroles. It is just part of the Wairakei geothermal system, the largest geothermal field in New Zealand, where underground hot water occurs at depths of less than 500 metres over an area of at least 40 square kilometres. Karapiti occupies a site which, until recently, boasted only one major fumarole, called Karapiti, and it owes its markedly increased activity directly to the exploitation of the geothermal field by the Wairakei Geothermal Power Station.

The Taupo Volcanic Zone has the greatest concentration of geothermal fields in New Zealand. They occur because in this area the crust reaches a temperature of at least 350°C at a depth of less than five kilometres. Ground water, infiltrating from above, is heated (but due to the pressure at this depth does not boil), then driven upwards by convection, often along faults or other cracks in the crust. At shallow depths boiling occurs, and a steam-water mixture results which finds its way to the surface by whatever routes are available to it.

Immediately below the ground surface of

the Wairakei geothermal field lies an
impermeable layer of rock which prevents the
termal waters below from reaching the
surface. At two major sites, however, this
barrier is thin or missing; at one (Karapiti) the
steam escapes while the other (Geyser Valley)
formerly discharged the hot water.

Over the years the bores of the power
station have lowered the level of the hot water
by approximately 300 metres. The result is
that very little hot water now reaches the
surface but, below the impervious 'lid', the hot
water has been replaced by a greatly increased
volume of steam. Thus, at Karapiti, activity
has steadily increased (although the original
fumarole has stopped, probably for natural
reasons) and new fumaroles frequently erupt,
often with no warning. Where steam
condenses at shallow depths, the soil is
liquified and a mud pool results. Those at
Karapiti are among the most violent in the
country.

In honour of its increased tourist potential,
Karapiti has been renamed 'Craters of the
Moon'. Unfortunately for the tourist trade, the
Wairakei Power Station — which requires
steam, not hot water, for its turbines — is
now tapping the newly-created steam reservoir
so that the present activity of the area could
well decline in the future.

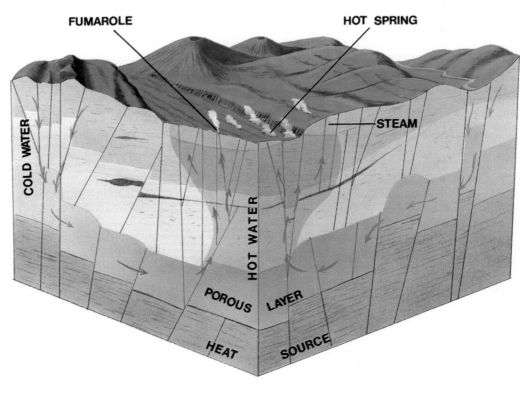

3. Land of domes and craters

Sixty kilometres north of Taupo lie the adjacent volcanic centres of Rotorua and Okataina. The latter is a centre of considerable complexity. Within its convoluted caldera (the result of many eruptions) lie not only lakes such as Rotoiti, Rotoehu, Rotoma, Tarawera and Okataina itself, but also large dome volcanoes such as Haroharo and Tarawera. Rotorua, in contrast, is the Taupo Volcanic Zone's only single-event caldera — a fact reflected in the simple, roughly circular shape of the lake and of the surrounding crater.

Rotorua
To the south, east and north, the perimeter of the 20 kilometre-diameter Rotorua caldera is clearly marked by an approximately circular fault scarp — the result of the area within the caldera dropping downwards. To the west, however, it seems the earth's surface bent rather than broke, since the land slopes gently to the lake. The lake level has, in the past, been up to 90 metres higher than it is at present, but it has developed only since the eruption, 140,000 years ago, that created the caldera. Rotorua erupted on dry land, and thus the pyroclastic flows were hot enough to form a thick welded ignimbrite — the youngest such ignimbrite in the entire area.

The eruption was vast. Over 300 cubic kilometres of ignimbrite were produced which, pouring out to the west, covered more than 3,000 square kilometres of land and formed a distinctive, dark pink rock, peppered with grey-white pumice fragments, which geologists call the Mamaku Ignimbrite. A further 200 cubic

A Haast's eagle (Harpagornis moorei) flies high above a scene of utter devastation — the Rotorua caldera less than half a century after its eruption. Approximately concentric fault scarps ring the crater from the centre of which rises a dome volcano. In time this dome will be totally buried beneath lake sediments and the debris of other eruptions; today it lies beneath the southern end of the lake and Rotorua city. Not so the other erupting volcano visible in this view. It is Mount Ngongotaha, which stands today to the west of the city. Other dome volcanoes such as Mokoia Island and a few small hills on the south eastern lake shore were probably erupted almost 100,000 years later.

Haast's eagle, with a wingspan of up to 2.8 metres and a weight of 9 to 13 kilograms, was the largest eagle in the world. Unique to New Zealand, it probably fed principally on moas. It became extinct only a few hundred years ago.

kilometres of material never escaped the caldera. Immediately after the eruption there was a period of rhyolitic dome building which created Mount Ngongotaha and another dome volcano, now almost totally buried beneath Rotorua city, but no further major eruptions. Later pyroclastic eruptions from the nearby Okataina centre — in particular one from the vicinity of Lake Rotoiti 50,000 years ago — wrought some changes upon the Rotorua caldera, but on the whole it has remained intact to the present day. Today the caldera is home to a number of active geothermal regions, but it is thought that they owe their existence to the presence of subterranean hot rocks rather than a large body of magma: the Rotorua volcanic centre is probably extinct.

Okataina
The same can certainly not be said of the Okataina volcanic centre. The region is bounded by a large but very irregularly-shaped caldera, the result of numerous relatively small but extremely violent pyroclastic eruptions. Since the last major outburst, rhyolitic dome building on a scale not seen elsewhere in the Taupo Volcanic Zone has obliterated the caldera floor and created not only sizable mountains but also numerous lakes.

The Okataina centre has produced at least five catastrophic pyroclastic and ignimbrite eruptions during the last 250,000 years, the last coming from an unknown vent somewhere near the eastern end of Lake Rotoiti about 50,000 years ago. Since then the area has been far from quiet. Between 40,000 and 25,000 years ago, there were nine large eruptions, four of particular violence, then, from 20,000 to 5,000 years ago, a series of eruptions with small pyroclastic flows built the dome volcano of Mount Haroharo and several other domes in the vicinity as well as the volcanoes around Lake Okareka. The lake itself, together with Lakes Tikitapu and Rotokakahi, lies in a basin formed by subsidence. At about the same time, a series of eruptions began the construction of Mount Tarawera, a process which continued until only 700 years ago. The mountain dammed a river valley, and the water backed up to create Lake Tarawera.

It is interesting that, for the last 25,000 years, all eruptions have occurred along two south-east to north-west trending fracture zones, each only a few kilometres wide, which presumably mark the location of two deep faults in the earth's crust below. Indeed, all eruptions in this time have been fissure eruptions, with several vents erupting either simultaneously or one after another along

Hailed as the eighth wonder of the world during the 40 or so years they were known to Western man, the Pink and White Terraces were the most spectacular features of a plethora of geothermal phenomena lining the shores of an otherwise nondescript lake of warm, dull-green water. The smaller Pink Terrace, or Otukapuarangi (cloud in the heavens), descended as a series of siliceous sinter steps from a deep spring of clear, turquoise-coloured hot water at the top. Much larger, the White Terrace or Te Tarata (the tattooed rock), rose 30 metres up the hillside and covered about three hectares (over seven acres). At each step there was a series of shallow pools with raised, cup-like lips. Hot water was supplied by an awesome boiling cauldron, again of clear, blue water. At irregular intervals, the water mysteriously withdrew from this cauldron, leaving it dry for several hours before fountaining back through the vent in its base to fill it once more.

The terraces became a popular tourist attraction during the mid-1800s, with visitors being rowed across the lake in whale boats manned by local Maoris, who acted as guides. After their destruction in the eruption of 1886 and the subsequent flooding of the entire valley (see map), they achieved almost mythological status. Artists such as Charles Blomfield, who had spent some weeks sketching and painting the terraces in the summer of 1884/1885, found an inexhaustible demand for paintings of them, with the result that he was turning out romantic, but essentially accurate, views until well into this century. This illustration, which looks across Lake Rotomahana from the Pink Terrace to the White

Terrace and Mount Tarawera, is based principally on a photograph taken by Charles Spencer in the 1880s and a 1912 painting by Blomfield.

Sinter deposits

The terraces were the largest sinter deposits in New Zealand, but virtually every geothermal region possesses smaller examples, the best remaining of which can be found at Orakeikorako and Waiotapu. Hot water, percolating through the silica-rich subterranean rock of the Taupo Volcanic Zone, dissolves the silica, which is carried in solution to the surface. Here, as the water cools, it is precipitated as sinter. Normally white or cream in colour, traces of antiminite and arsenic were responsible for the pinkish colour of Otukapuarangi. The same minerals in different concentration cause the yellow rim of the Champagne Pool at Waiotapu. Algae living in the hot water can also produce a variety of colours including the green, brown and black sinter that can be seen at Orakeikorako.

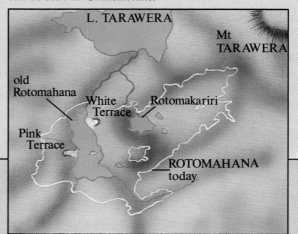

17

straight lines from one to 14 kilometres in length. This is nowhere more clearly illustrated than in the most violent recent eruption in New Zealand, that of Mount Tarawera on 10 June, 1886.

The Tarawera eruption

Prior to the eruption of 1886, Tarawera was a typical rhyolite dome volcano complex with a number of large, overlapping, flat-topped domes. It lay along the eastern margin of the Okataina caldera and to the south-west was a deep valley with two small lakes, called Rotomakariri and Rotomahana, a swamp and a couple of pools within it. Rotomahana was a warm lake, lying above an active geothermal system, and on its shores were two of the most remarkable products of geothermal activity to be found anywhere in the world: the Pink and White Terraces.

Built over thousands of years by the silica deposits from geothermal springs high on the valley side, both terraces fell as a series of sinter steps and pools to the lake shore. Even in the mid-nineteenth century the Terraces were recognised as a major tourist site and many New Zealand colonists and visitors made the arduous journey into the interior to view them. It is as well that the eruption occurred in mid-winter or the death toll could have been far higher.

There was little warning of an impending eruption — just a slight increase in geothermal activity (including unpredictable and sometimes violent explosions from the cauldron of the White Terrace) and, more ominously, mysterious, sudden changes in the water level of Lake Tarawera on two occasions. There was also a phantom canoe, reported by a group of Maoris and Europeans who were crossing Lake Tarawera by boat on their way to Lake Rotomahana and the Terraces. However, none of these signs — natural or supernatural — was interpreted as presaging a volcanic eruption from the apparently extinct Mount Tarawera. It was therefore a total surprise when, at about 1.30 am on 10 June 1886, an enormous cloud of ash and vapour rose from the mountain's summit (Ruawahia). Fifteen minutes later, the eruption commenced with a roar and a towering black eruption cloud arose, shot through with red reflections from the red-hot scoria being ejected from the crater. At this stage the volcanic vent was probably only 10 metres wide, but at 2.10 am the summit of Tarawera exploded with a deafening noise and a violent earthquake. By 2.30 am the whole length of the summit (five kilometres) was in eruption.

Activity began in the Rotomahana valley at 3.30 am with explosive eruptions from both lakes sending up a column of steam and mud higher than the cloud from Tarawera. It was from here, where lake water could react with the hot lava, that the most devastating eruptions came. At the same time, the violence of the eruption from the mountain increased still further, with blocks up to two metres in diameter being thrown from the fissures.

By 5.30 am, the main eruption was largely over, although south-west of Rotomahana in the Waimungu Valley activity was only just beginning, and continued sporadically for a month. Here, however, while the initial eruptions were volcanic, later explosions appear to have been largely steam-generated (phreatic eruptions).

The results of the eruption were far-reaching. The death toll was at least 150, two villages being totally buried. Lake Tarawera, its outflow blocked, rose by a metre, then subsequently slowly fell again until, in 1904, this dam suddenly gave way and flooded the area downstream. Along the summit of the mountain was a series of craters up to 150 metres deep and 200 metres wide. This rift extended to the outer slopes in the south-west, where 'The Chasm' had been formed, then on into the Rotomahana valley. Here at first there was no lake at all, but a rift of awesome proportions, in which a new lake began to form within a month.

Of the Pink and White Terraces there was no sign, and the geography of the region was so much altered (the surface of the new lake, for example, being at the bottom of a crater, was fully 160 metres lower than the old Rotomahana) that visitors had difficulty in even establishing where they once lay. In time, a second lake formed in the valley, and the water levels of both rose until they joined to form the present Lake Rotomahana, filling the entire valley.

Waimungu thermal region

Further south-west, the Waimungu Valley became New Zealand's youngest and most violent thermal region. Although it had not been a geothermal region prior to 1886, it seems that the geothermal system beneath Rotomahana extended underground into the valley. The initial basaltic eruptions, immediately after the main event, produced a number of small, steep-sided craters, running up the valley and aligned with the Tarawera rift. Although these remained active for some weeks, activity gradually subsided to a low level that persisted for several years. Then in late 1900 a violent hydrothermal eruption occurred at the north end of Echo Crater. The area

After the destruction of two of the most beautiful sinter deposits in the world by the largest modern eruption in New Zealand came the world's largest 'geyser'. For four years, from 1900 to 1904, the Waimungu Geyser (actually not a geyser in the accepted sense at all, but a site of violent hydrothermal eruptions, the explosions probably originating from several hundred metres down) erupted to heights of up to 450 metres from a pool in Echo Crater. Today only a shallow puddle of hot water remains, half hidden amidst stunted manuka trees.

today takes its name from it, for Waimungu means 'black water', and the Waimungu Geyser typically erupted muddy water and blocks of solid material. Its behaviour was unpredictable, with the result that several sight-seers lost their lives to it. Sometimes it would lie quiescent for days on end, only to explode suddenly into violent eruption. Sometimes it would erupt to heights of 150 metres for hours, and occasionally up to 450 metres. The Waimungu Geyser continued in this way until, on 1 November, 1904, it fell silent, never to erupt again.

Nearby Frying-pan Flat exploded without warning on 1 April 1917, and sent a mud and rock-loaded steam cloud rolling up the valley to lift the roof off the Waimungu Accommodation House, close to the present tea kiosk, 800 metres away. Two of its three occupants were scalded to death. For the rest of the day explosions threw solid material up to 300 metres and, for three following days, ejecta

burst through the billowing steam to heights of 120 metres. Within two weeks of the eruption, hot water was collecting in the new crater and eventually formed Frying-pan Lake, now renamed the Waimungu Cauldron. Smaller hydrothermal eruptions occurred in the cauldron on 22 February 1973 when, in 15 minutes, about 970 cubic metres of rock were ejected from a vent just offshore, and about 2 May 1981, when two small craters were excavated in Raupo Pond Crater.

Today the full 14 kilometre length of this eruption is easily accessible to the public. Waimungu Valley is open to visitors, and regular boat trips on Lake Rotomahana leave from the foot of the valley to view what is left of the pre-eruption thermal area. Tarawera's vast craters can be reached by foot or four-wheel drive vehicle from the south-east, while for the more energetic, there is the longer, less well-defined climb from the shores of Lake Tarawera up the north-western slopes.

Whakarewarewa geothermal area

Perhaps the most famous of New Zealand's geothermal areas, Whakarewarewa, within the Rotorua caldera close to both the lake and the city, boasts the highest density of geysers in the world. Geysers occur where a hot spring with a relatively small outlet is connected to a considerably larger subterranean chamber. There may be several interconnecting chambers and geysers, as is the case at Whakarewarewa.

Hot water and cooler surface water seep into the chamber, slowly filling it and the exit tube above it. Throughout its height, the column of water remains just below the boiling point for that pressure. Eventually, however, the slow rate of cooling or the diminishing input of cold surface water as the level rises means that the upper layers flash to steam and boil violently away. The removal of this surface layer reduces the pressure in the

Photograph by Manfred Hochstein

entire liquid column, and sudden boiling moves downwards until it reaches the bottom of the chamber. As the water boils, there is a dramatic increase in pressure, forcing water and steam through the one escape route available at high speed: the geyser erupts.

On the night of 10 June 1886, New Zealanders, Maori and colonist alike, received a sharp demonstration of the powers that lurked beneath the North Island when the supposedly extinct Mount Tarawera and neighbouring Lake Rotomahana erupted. Although the eruption was relatively small — only 0.1 cubic kilometres of material was ejected and it was largely over in four hours — it is, nonetheless, the largest eruption to have occurred in historic times. Ash fell as far away as Wellington, 370 kilometres to the south, and it was heard in Picton, 400 kilometres away. In Auckland, 200 kilometres from the eruption, it was loud enough to bring people from their beds and was initially commonly thought to be a Russian attack upon the city or, in view of the occasional flashes that could be seen and the lack of falling shells, a warship in distress on the Manukau Bar. Earthquakes and hydrothermal eruptions from Rotomahana and the Waimungu Valley continued for some months after the main eruption, but initial fears that it was but the start of more prolonged activity proved unfounded. Today, Mount Tarawera, split from end to end in one night, again appears extinct and the new Lake Rotomahana retains only some steaming cliffs and a water temperature 4°C above that of neighbouring Lake Tarawera (itself a lake with some thermal activity) as a reminder of the thermal field which now lies drowned beneath it.

4. Sentinels of the North and South

The active volcanoes of Ruapehu and White Island mark the southern and northern extremities of the Taupo Volcanic Zone. Each is one of a group of andesitic volcanoes clustered at either end of the zone. Thus, to the south of White Island are Motuhora (Whale Island), Manawahe and Edgecumbe, while to the north of Ruapehu are the active peaks of Ngauruhoe and Tongariro, the extinct Kakaramea and Pihanga, and several smaller cones.

Northern group

The heavily eroded state of Manawahe attests to its great age; it is in fact 750,000 years old. Mount Edgecumbe, on the other hand, is relatively young. Its 821 metre-high cone was created by eruptions from several vents. The summit of the main cone is flat, apart from two small explosion craters, while two large domes at the western foot of the main cone record an episode when lava more viscous than usual was extruded. Edgecumbe was last active from 5500 to 3500 years ago, and while at present it appears totally devoid of life (geothermal activity at nearby Kawerau is at least 200,000 years old, and thus has nothing to do with the volcano), it may not yet be extinct.

Motuhora lies eight kilometres offshore from Whakatane, and is the summit of a submarine volcano. It consists of an eroded cone which rises 348 metres above sea level flanked by two domes. The known age of various ash deposits from mainland sources that have covered this volcano suggests it is at least 50,000 years old. The western dome may be younger since the oldest ash covering it is only 9000 years old, but older material may have been eroded away prior to this. Between the cone and the east dome a few fumaroles, an area of heated ground and some near-boiling springs in the intertidal zone of Brimstone Bay, are all that is left of a once more extensive geothermal field.

White Island

In marked contrast, White Island, 48 kilometres offshore, is the most active volcano in New Zealand. Indeed, its name derives from the plume of white steam which generally rises high above the summit. On a clear day it is visible from the Bay of Plenty coast; for those who want a closer inspection helicopter trips leave from both Whakatane and Rotorua, weather and volcano permitting.

The island is merely the crater rim of a 700 metre-high submarine volcano. Most of its area is occupied by the 0.5 by 1.25 kilometre Main Crater. This is actually formed from three adjacent subcraters, the most easterly of which is open to the sea while the volcano's active vents are clustered at the opposite end. White Island's history prior to the arrival of Europeans in New Zealand is unknown, although we know it is at least 16,000 years old, but since the first recorded visit to the island in 1826 it has erupted frequently and violently.

In the early days, boiling lakes lay in the several smaller craters which occupied the Main Crater floor. The largest of these was drained in 1899 to assist sulphur mining operations and, for some years after this, sulphur miners actually lived on the island. In 1914, however, part of the south-west wall of the Main Crater collapsed into the western subcrater where it mixed with steam to produce an avalanche of debris which swept down the Main Crater, overwhelming all 11 miners and destroying the buildings at the eastern end. Mining was subsequently resumed, although never again did anyone live on the island, and by 1934, when operations finally ceased, some 10,000 tonnes of sulphur had been removed.

Since 1914, White Island has erupted more than 20 times, creating a series of new vents which, through landslips and further eruptions, have changed shape and coalesced to form the crater floor as it is today. The largest historical eruption occurred between December 1976 and December 1981, when two major craters were formed (called the 1978 Crater Complex) and about 0.1 cubic kilometres of rock were erupted. Subsequently new vents have continued to appear which, together with older ones, continuously pour forth an acrid mixture of steam, acid, sulphur and ash. While this is for the most part accomplished in an eerie silence, one vent, appropriately named Noisy Nelly, thunders like a huge furnace as it emits gases so hot that only the shimmering of the air above the 10 metre-diameter hole betrays their existence. In fact, temperatures of more than 500°C have been recorded for this vent, causing surrounding rock to become incandescent at night.

White Island owes its spectacular activity to two phenomena. Firstly, a shallow geothermal sytem, fed by rainfall (for White Island is impervious to the sea), lies beneath the island. This produces the mud pools, voluminous steam and earlier boiling lakes. Secondly, vents such as Noisy Nelly are chimneys up which gases escape directly from the magma chamber many kilometres below. In the circumstances, it comes as a surprise to discover not only vegetation (albeit often dead) clinging to the island's outer slopes, but even a thriving gannet

White Island in active mood in February 1989. During the first few months of the year two new vents opened in the western subcrater, and mild ash eruptions were an almost hourly occurrence, interspersed with more violent explosions every few days. In this view, from due south, the western subcrater occupies the middle of the island, with the other two subcraters which make up the Main Crater extending to the right. To the left is the eroded remnant of an older cone.

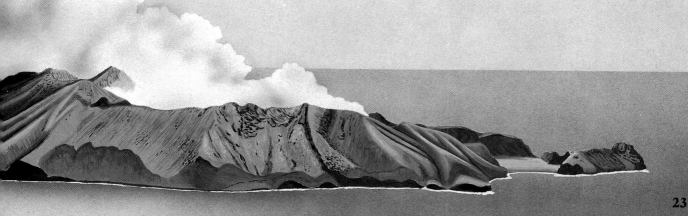

colony. White Island is unlike any other New Zealand volcano; indeed, there can be few places on earth similar to it. A visit to the island is an unforgettable experience, but one which few would care to prolong!

Southern group

Compared with White Island, the volcanoes of the Tongariro volcano centre, at the other end of the Taupo Volcanic Zone, appear almost benign. It is, however, a false impression.

The age of the Tongariro volcanoes is unknown, but is of the order of half a million years. The oldest dated lava flows are only about half that age, but they give little clue to the true antiquity of the mountains as they almost certainly overlie older flows. The dates of final eruptions can be equally difficult to pin down. The cones of Kakaramea and Kuharua, close to the shore of Lake Taupo, are overlaid by debris from that volcano's eruption 22,000 years ago, and so have been extinct for at least that long. Pihanga, on the other hand, has several cones which have no such covering, implying activity in the last 22,000 years.

Tongariro

This massive and complex volcano is the result of eruptions from at least 12 cones, the youngest and most active of which is Ngauruhoe. Like all the volcanoes in this group, its shape has been substantially altered by glacial erosion during the last Ice Age, while eruptions, too, have partially destroyed the mountain during its long life so that today's cones are all relatively young features. Among the oldest are Tama lakes, Blue Lake Crater and North Crater, all of which erupted during a period of intense activity about 10,000 years ago.

Most of the younger flows on Tongariro itself have come from Red Crater, although its most recent eruptions in 1855 and 1926, and possibly between 1885 and 1890, were explosive and produced no lava. Upper Te Maari Crater also erupted explosively in the late 1800s, proving that age does not necessarily mean extinction — the last eruption from that area had been from lower Te Maari Crater almost 14,000 years previously.

Today, steam is discharged from a number of areas on the volcano (including both Red and Te Maari craters) but, unlike that of neighbouring Ngauruhoe, it is not of magmatic origin for, almost uniquely, Tongariro has a geothermal system beneath it (see panel on page 27).

The Main Crater of White Island in 1989. Ash and steam billow continuously from the western subcrater, while smaller vents emit steam in the central subcrater area.

The broad pile of Ruapehu gives little clue to this volcano's activity for the vent is submerged beneath a lake. Crater Lake was, at the time this photograph was taken in February 1989, erupting hydrothermally every three or four days.

Despite its size, Ruapehu is a relatively easy volcano to climb, the summit plateau being reached after only two to three hours' walk across lava flows and glaciers from the carpark at Top of the Bruce. In winter chair lifts shorten the distance still further, although snow increases the difficulty of the remaining climb.

Ngauruhoe in eruption in 1975. For many years lava-producing eruptions alternated with periods of explosive activity, culminating in two large ash eruptions in early 1974 and 1975. During the latter, the eruption cloud at times reached about 13 kilometres above the summit, small pyroclastic flows swept down the mountain flanks, and incandescent scoria could be seen fountaining in the vent. Violent explosions were heard more than 80 kilometres away, and threw blocks of lava up to three kilometres from the summit. — (Photograph reproduced by kind permission of Tongariro National Park.)

Ngauruhoe

Ngauruhoe commenced eruption about 2500 years ago, and was largely built over the following 700 years, although it has probably been more or less continuously active ever since. It appears to occupy the site of a much older (260,000 years old) and larger cone which was eroded by glacial action during the last Ice Age. More than 60 eruptions have been recorded since 1839, and while most have been small-scale ash eruptions, lava flowed from the crater in 1870, 1949 and 1954. The last eruption was the largest. Between June and September, 10 lava flows poured down the north-west slopes while lava fountains in the crater built up a cinder cone which formed the basis of the present cone within the crater. Since then, several small, explosive eruptions have occurred, building to a climax in 1974 and 1975, after which eruptions abruptly ceased.

Although steam still rises from the bottom of Ngauruhoe's crater, it is rarely visible above the rim. To see it one must reach the summit, a frustrating climb of about an hour on steep scree-covered or (in winter) snow-covered slopes. The mountain is most readily approached from the west, where the Mangatepopo Road brings one to within an hour or two's walk of its base.

Ruapehu

This volcano is responsible for New Zealand's worst railway disaster. On Christmas Eve, 1953, an avalanche of water, ash and boulders swept down the mountainside into the Whangaehu River. Shortly before 11.00 pm, it reached the railway bridge at Tangiwai and swept it away. When the Wellington-Auckland express reached the bridge only a few minutes later, the locomotive, tender and six carriages plunged into the river. One carriage was carried approximately 2.4 kilometres downstream and 151 people were killed.

Where did this lethal mud flow — so different from our conception of 'normal' volcanic products — come from? The answer is from the very summit of the mountain, for in Ruapehu's crater lies a lake.

At least six craters can be distinguished on the complex summit of this volcano. Only one is currently active, and is filled with a near-circular lake, 500 metres across. This lake, more than 180 metres deep, hides a volcanic vent not unlike that of White Island. Hot magmatic gases are discharged into the water at such a rate that, despite the vast surface area and the fact that it is well above the snow line, the lake normally has a surface temperature of about 40°C while, not far below, the temperature is well over 100°C. The gas discharge is erratic, however. Sometimes the lake cools, while at other times it heats up so much that parts of it exceed the boiling point. If only a small portion near the surface is involved, the result is a spectacular but relatively harmless hydrothermal eruption. If, however, a large volume of water, including that at depth, boils, water mixed with mud and boulders from the lake bed is hurled out onto the flanks of the volcano. Here, further loose ash, boulders and melted snow may be incorporated and a devastating mud flow, called a *lahar*, rolls down the mountainside. Ruapehu's history is filled with such flows. Indeed, the first time European observers noted activity from the volcano was when a lahar flooded the Whangaehu river in 1861. It was not until 1878 that the crater lake was first seen.

Ketetahi hot springs

High on the slopes of Mount Tongariro lie Ketetahi hot springs which, together with steaming ground at Red Crater and Te Maari Craters, also on Tongariro, represent the highest thermal field in New Zealand. Unlike other thermal regions — where, as we have seen, hot water from deep below the earth separates into steam and water near the surface — at the Tongariro thermal field the lowest levels, deep in the heart of the mountain, are of steam, which cools to a hot water/steam mixture as it rises. At Ketetahi and Red Crater, however, in addition to hot springs, there are fumaroles which apparently discharge steam directly from this deep layer. One at Ketetahi releases steam from the ground at a temperature of 138°C and at a speed of more than 90 metres per second.

Ketetahi springs are two hours' climb from the carpark by State Highway 47, north of the

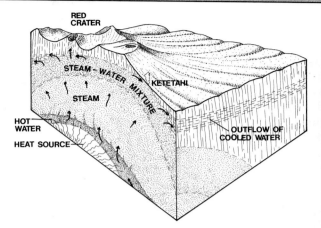

mountain. With a hut of the same name nearby, they provide an excellent starting point for the exploration of Tongariro's complex summit. On a clear day, the view from either springs or hut must be one of the most magnificent in the world.

More devastating even than the eruption which led up to it, a huge avalanche cascades down the north-western slopes of Ruapehu and out onto the surrounding ring plain about 9700 years ago. The avalanche was preceded by a major period of cone construction involving the 'Dome Crater' which, through earthquakes and increased hydrothermal activity, weakened mountain flanks that had already been rendered unstable by lava flows and ash falls. Eventually, about 0.2 cubic kilometres of the upper slopes of the volcano collapsed and the avalanche poured down the Wairere and Whakapapanui stream valleys to a distance of more than 12 kilometres from the volcano.

Today, the debris from this avalanche is at least 12 metres thick over much of the area, thinning to about one metre at the margins. However, the most striking relics of the collapse are the numerous mounds, some up to 10 metres high, which can be seen from State Highways 47 and 48 (the road to Whakapapa and Iwikau villages). Many of these have as their basis large

blocks of rock from the mountainside which were rafted along in the avalanche. Subsequently, several lahars have followed the same course as the dry debris avalanche, depositing their load of mud and rock over it.

Glacial erosion and many eruptions have so altered the appearance of Ruapehu during the millenia since the event that any attempt to reconstruct the mountain as it appeared then is largely conjectural. In this illustration a small cone is shown above what today is no more than a shallow depression of the summit area, called Dome Crater. Less uncertain is the thick snow mantle shown, for the avalanche occurred not long after the last Ice Age, when permanent snow and glaciers extended far down the mountain, and the surrounding plain was snow-covered in winter. The glaciers on Ruapehu have been in retreat ever since and, as early photographs and accounts clearly demonstrate, the withdrawal has been particularly rapid over the last 50 years.

At first it was, as it is today, a hot water lake but, after a few years of ash and steam eruptions, the lake cooled and finally froze in 1926. Eruptions recommenced in 1934 and the lake thawed, only to be totally replaced by a dome of lava that rose as an island in March 1945. Later that same year the dome was destroyed by explosions, and by early 1946 a boiling lake had appeared at the bottom of the 300 metre-deep crater. The water level rose, and by December 1953 was eight metres higher than its old level, the overflow having been blocked by ice and ash. It was the collapse of that dam, and the rapid release of thousands of cubic metres of hot water, that precipitated the Tangiwai disaster.

Since then Ruapehu has erupted through its crater lake at least four times, generating lahars on every occasion. The lahars of two eruptions, in 1969 and 1975, severely damaged kiosks and chair lifts in the ski resort of Whakapapa. It was only the fact that the eruptions happened at night and out of the skiing season that prevented fatalities. Ruapehu's most recent eruption was in 1977. Since then the mountain has been silent, but its status as the North Island's most popular winter tourist resort confers upon it the potential for a disaster of major proportions.

Ngauruhoe today, viewed from the east; looks may deceive.

Postscript
The volcanoes of the Tongariro area are the best known of the many in the Taupo Volcanic Zone. However, as we have seen, they are neither the most active nor the largest. They will undoubtedly continue to erupt from time to time in the years ahead but, as Tarawera demonstrated in 1886, the next major New Zealand eruption may well not involve them at all. The real giants will probably slumber for a few more centuries yet — but when they awake, all New Zealand will feel the awesome power of the Taupo Volcanic Zone.

Selected bibliography

To give a full reference list would serve little purpose in a book such as this. However, there are a number of excellent publications that can be recommended to those wanting to learn more about the Taupo Volcanic Zone.

For an up-to-date history of New Zealand from earliest times to the present day there can be no book better than *Prehistoric New Zealand*, by Graeme Stevens, Matt McGlone and Beverley McCulloch, published in 1988 by Heinemann Reed.

Readers wanting further information specifically on the Taupo Volcanic Zone will find that no book for the general reader other than this one covers the entire area. However, *Geyserland: a guide to the Volcanoes and Geothermal Areas of Rotorua*, by B. F. Houghton, published by the Geological Society of New Zealand (Guidebook 4) in 1982, is a useful account of the Rotorua and Okataina centres; while *Volcanoes of the South Wind*, by Karen Williams, published by the Tongariro Natural History Society, covers the cones of the Tongariro centre in well-illustrated detail. For the reader prepared to tackle the complexities of scientific writing, there are a number of publications on the entire region, among which *Active Volcanoes and Geothermal Systems, Taupo Volcanic Zone, International Volcanological Congress 1987*, published by the New Zealand Geological Survey (Record 22) is one of the most complete.